TRANSFORMING ✥ TRADITIONS

VOLUME 1 | AUTUMN 2009

# BEGINNINGS:

## Children's Stories From Matthew and Genesis

*Edited by Elizabeth Caldwell and Theodore Hiebert*

TRANSFORMING ✛ TRADITIONS

VOLUME 1 | AUTUMN 2009

# Table of Contents

*Featured Course: Reading the Bible With Children and Youth*

# It began over dinner.

We were working on a children's story based on Ted's new interpretation of the story of Babel in Genesis 11:1-9 and Lib's adaptation of the story for children. We were trying to figure out how to make the most rigorous biblical analysis accessible in the most straightforward way. Then it hit us: this is the task of the Seminary. This is the core of theological education: transforming traditions. This is exactly what we want our students to learn to do as well as possible, because this is what their ministry is all about.

Before dinner was over, we had designed a new course: *Reading the Bible with Children and Youth.* Our aim was to have each student do solid biblical study, a thorough interpretation of a biblical story as the first audience would have heard it, and then to ask them to tell this story to a specific modern audience, taking account of both the cultural differences and human commonalities between these two audiences. We believed this process would not only help students practice the kind of transformation of traditions that is at the heart of all ministry, but that it would produce some new and fresh Bible stories, told in new ways for the first time.

This book includes 12 of the stories written by the members of this class. In one way or another they tell familiar biblical stories in ways they have never been told before, because they are so careful to take account of both the historical and modern audiences of these stories. We are excited to make them available to a wider audience. We hope that even the youngest among us will grow up with the ability to hear, interpret, retell, and learn from the stories of our faith.

– *Professors Lib Caldwell & Ted Hiebert*

# Imagine

*by Nathan Soule-Hill*

### AUTHOR'S STATEMENT

**GENESIS 1:1-2:4A** *Imagine* is an invitation to be immersed in the wonder of God's creativity. The Biblical creation narratives are vital resources in shaping how Christians think about God and the world; and this story asks its listeners to employ their own creativity as they imagine the creation anew. Although appropriate for any age group, the text reads at a 3rd grade level.

In *Imagine*, the value of every human being and the call to be faithful caretakers of the Earth are important themes. But above all, the story centers on the marvel that is God's creation. Giving children the opportunity to engage their own imaginations as they think about God's past and on-going activity in the world, in the universe, and even in themselves is what this story is all about!

**NATHAN SOULE-HILL** is a 2009 graduate of McCormick. A native of Red Bluff, California, the beauty of the Sacramento Valley instilled in him a passion for caring for God's creation.

*This story was illustrated by Jennifer Soule-Hill. Jennifer is a 2007 graduate of McCormick and an ordained minister in the Presbyterian Church (USA). Her work as an activist on the U.S.-Mexico border exposed her to the artwork of Peter Parnell, and his desert landscapes serve as the inspiration for her illustrations.*

*Nathan and Jennifer currently serve as co-pastors of the Family of Christ Presbyterian Church in Greeley, Colorado.*

At the beginning of everything,
    there is only One thing...
And that One thing
    is the center of everything.
God created you.
    I know because
    God created me too.
You are God's child.

Can you imagine it?
    What would it be like if you remembered the
    moment when you were created?
How did God make you special?
    What did God say to you?

When I imagine that moment,
    I think God held me close, looked at my face,
    and said to me, "You are my child; you are very good."

(That's what God says to all of us.)

In the beginning...
...was God's creativity!

4

Can you imagine God creating your parents? What about your grandparents? They were children once too, you know. And when they were little kids, and when they became grown ups, the whole time they were God's children.

How many kids do you think God has created? More than anyone can count, I bet.

Imagine how long ago God created the very first people. God must have been so happy when God saw the first children. God loves little boys and girls. When God first saw them, God must have said, "You are very good!"

But can you imagine the world before there were people? What do you think God created then? I bet it was the animals.

God made them all: the giraffe and the hippopotamus, the cows and the sheep, the squirrel and the deer, the birds and the fish, the dogs and the cats, even the worms and the bugs!

And God loved them too. God looked at them all and said, "You are very good!"

**But can you imagine the world before there were people or animals?**

What do you think God created then? I bet it was the plants and the trees. God made them all – the flowers and the grass, the cornstalk and the apple tree, the fern and the mushroom, even the cactus and the Venus fly trap! And God loved them too. God looked at them all and said, "You are very good!"

But can you imagine the world before there were people or animals or plants? What do you think God created then? It must have been the rest of the world.

God made it all – the ground and the air, the sea and the sky, the sun and the moon, the stars and the clouds, even the light of the daytime.
   And God loved it all. God looked at the world and said, "You are very good!"

**"You are very good!"**

6

Before there were people or animals, before there were fish or birds, before there were plants or trees, before there was sea or sky, even before there was sun and moon,

*Can you imagine it??*

(Close your eyes for a moment.)

Imagine the world before it was created. It was just a mixed-up jumble of what was yet to be.

But God was there. God's Spirit was moving upon the Earth. God's Spirit is like the wind or a breath of air. And when God's Spirit touched the Earth, the world began to move.

*Can you imagine it?*

Things begin to move and to take form. Imagine it! How do you imagine the creativity?

(You can open your eyes now.)

What shapes can you see?

What colors begin to jump?

Can you see waves upon the water?

Are plants beginning to grow?

Can you see new creations with each passing second?

It all began with God's creativity. God's creativity made the world. God's creativity made you. That is why you are God's child.

God says to you, "My child, you are special. Look at the world around you. I have created the sea and the land, the plants and the trees, the fish and the birds, the animals and people.

I love them all, they are all very good. Please take care of them for me. This will be a very big task because the world is so big. But never forget, I love the Earth, and I need you to love the Earth too."

And when God was done saying all this, God was very tired. So God took a rest. But even as God rested creation kept happening. The trees grew taller and the chickens hatched chicklets. The people built cities, invented languages, made music and had families.

God's creativity never stops! God, who loves us, invites us to create too. So imagine what will be created next. Imagine how you will create with God.

And always remember to imagine!

8

# The Garden of Eden

*by Eric Heinekamp*

## AUTHOR'S STATEMENT

GENESIS 2:4B-3:24 My story is *The Garden of Eden*. I selected this tale because it is familiar but frequently misquoted and misused. I believe it is important for our youth to hear this story as it was written.

I have rewritten this story for youth between the ages of 6-10. The story is not targeted to any particular social or cultural audience.

My hope in retelling this story is to help readers imagine the very first encounters between God and humans. The primary value I present is that our loving God gives us rules but also gives us grace when we break those rules. As I say in the story, God always gives us a second chance.

The adaptation remains faithful to the ancient text but retells the story of the Garden of Eden from Adam's point of view as he tells his young sons, Cain and Abel, about where he used to live.

ERIC HEINEKAMP earned his Masters in Divinity from McCormick Seminary in May 2009. He is a member of Knox Presbyterian Church in Naperville, Illinois and is in the process of becoming a Minister of Word and Sacrament in the Presbyterian Church (USA). His goal is to work in parish ministry where he is particularly interested in teaching, church growth, and leadership within the denomination.

The Garden of Eden *was illustrated by several 8-10 year-old students at Knox Presbyterian Church in Naperville, Illinois. Special thanks go to Charlie, Matthew, Matt, Sara, Jessica, Evan, Mindy, Claire, and Abbi.*

**"Daddy, tell us your story again about where you used to live. The one about you and mommy in the garden."**

Cain and his brother Abel walked behind Adam patting down the dirt as their dad planted seeds in the hard ground. "And the snake! Don't forget about the snake!"

Adam laughed, "OK, OK, but just for a minute. We have work to do." They sat down in the dust and Adam told his story.

"Long ago, the world was a dry empty place. There were no people or animals or even plants. God didn't want to be alone and took some mud and formed it into the first person. Just like you play with clay, God molded the first man." Adam squished his hands in the dirt pretending to make a man. The boys did too. "Then God blew the breath of life into the mud man's nose and he came to life."

"That was you, right daddy?"

"Yes, Abel, that was me. God created a grassy garden by a river in a place called Eden. There were plants and flowers and fruit trees. God asked me to take care of the garden and gave me one important rule.
God said, 'You can eat anything except fruit from the Tree of Knowledge.'

"I liked the garden but it wasn't fun being by myself. God saw I was lonely and made wild animals and birds to be with me. I made up names for them like **kangaroo** and **monkey** and **giraffe**."

"Those are funny names" Cain said.

"But I was still lonely. When I was sleeping God took out one of my ribs," Adam tickled the boys' sides, "and created your mommy. When I woke up and saw her I was in love. I finally had my perfect partner."

"Mommy's name is Eve." Abel said proudly. The boys squirmed and looked at each other. Adam was coming to their favorite part.

"We were happy in the garden and had plenty of food and animal friends. We didn't wear any clothes but didn't even notice"

The boys giggled. "You were naked."

"Then one day a clever snake showed up. Snake asked mommy what God said about the fruit trees. She said we can eat any fruit except from that tree and she pointed to the tree in the middle of the garden."

The boys pointed, showing how mommy did it.

"Snake hissed, 'You can eat that fruit. God doesn't want you to eat it because it will make you as smart as God.'

"We were curious about what Snake said and walked closer to the tree. Mommy looked at the fruit and wondered what it meant to be as smart as God. It seemed harmless so she picked a ripe fruit, closed her eyes, and took a big bite. **CRUNCH!**

"The fruit was juicy and sweet. Mommy gave some to me and I ate it too. Just then we realized we did something wrong. I had a bad feeling in my stomach. We noticed we were naked and felt embarrassed. We broke God's one rule."

Were you sad, daddy?" Cain asked.

"Yes, we were both sad. And I thought God would be sad too.

"That evening we heard God walking in the garden so we hid in the bushes. God couldn't find us and called out, 'Where are you?'"

"You were hiding from God." The boys said.

"I called back. 'We're in the bushes because we are naked.' God asked, 'How do you know you are naked? Did you eat the forbidden fruit?'

"Then we made another mistake. I said, "It's not my fault. The partner you created gave me the fruit." And mommy said "It's not my fault either. The snake you created made me curious." We blamed each other and even blamed God. We didn't admit we did something wrong.

"Everything had changed. God said to Snake, 'Because you encouraged Eve to break my rule you are cursed. From now on snakes won't have legs and will crawl in the dust. And people will not like you.'

"God was disappointed that mommy and I broke the rule about the fruit and sad that we did not take responsibility for what we did. God told us we had learned a valuable lesson but it was time for us to leave the garden. God made us clothes and sent us here to give us a second chance.

"You see, God loves us even when we break God's rules. And God loves you too."

# Ishmael's Family Splits Apart

*Written and Illustrated by Kendra Grams*

## AUTHOR'S STATEMENT

**GENESIS 21:8-21** Many modern realities force families apart: divorce, disaster, war, incarceration, etc. In the midst of the fear and uncertainty caused by families splitting apart, children need to know that God is with them and will take care of them and their families. I wrote this story in the hope that children will find such a reassurance by hearing how God was with Ishmael when his family split. This story is designed to be read and discussed with children (Christian or Jewish) in grades 3-6, roughly ages 9-12. In order to make the story more accessible to children, I have told the story from Ishmael's perspective rather than using a narrator like the biblical text.

**KENDRA GRAMS** is a member of the Presbyterian Church (U.S.A.). She received her M.Div. from McCormick Theological Seminary in 2009. She grew up in rural Nebraska, but has come to love big-city life as well. She looks forward to a life-time of pastoral ministry, particular ministry with the young and marginalized.

**Being a family can be hard.** Sometimes people fight. Sometimes families even split. When I was a kid, my family split. It was really hard on me, and I think it was hard for my parents too. But we weren't alone.... Let me tell you the story.

One day, I was playing with my younger brother, Isaac. Well, actually, Isaac is my half brother. We have the same father, but different mothers. Anyway, his mother Sarah saw us playing together, and it seemed to upset her. I didn't know why. We were just playing.

Later, I found out why she was upset. I was walking outside my father Abraham's tent and overheard Sarah talking to my father. She said, "Send Ishmael and his mother Hagar away. My son Isaac shall not share your land and animals with Ishmael!" I was shocked!

16

That evening I saw my father, and he seemed really upset. When I walked by his tent on my way to bed, I heard him praying, "Oh God! What should I do? Ishmael is my son too." I think he was crying.

Early the next morning, my mother Hagar woke me up and said we were leaving. I asked where we were going, but she didn't answer. Outside my father Abraham was waiting for us. He gave my mother a bag of water and some bread.

Then my father bent down and gave me a big hug. Before he let me go, he said to me, "Don't worry. God said that God will take care of you."

When my father let go of me, my mother took my hand, and we walked away. I was really confused and scared. It felt like my family was falling apart completely.

My mother Hagar and I wandered around in the desert for a long time. After awhile, the water was gone. I got really thirsty. I think my mother was really thirsty too.

So she found a bush and left me there to rest in the shade. She went and rested under another bush nearby. I think she tried to go far enough away that I couldn't hear her crying, but I still heard her.

I began to cry too. I also said a prayer, but I was starting to think that God had forgotten us.

After awhile, my mother came, took my hand, and helped me up. She said, "God heard you! God is with us! God has shown me a well!"

Then she led me to the well. My mother filled the bag with water and gave me a drink. As I drank that water, I knew that God was with us and would take care of us.

And God did protect us and take care of us. My mother helped me as I grew up. She even found a wife for me. And now my wife and I have twelve sons of our own.

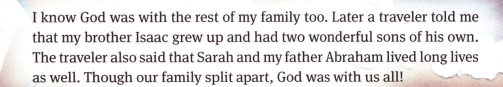

I know God was with the rest of my family too. Later a traveler told me that my brother Isaac grew up and had two wonderful sons of his own. The traveler also said that Sarah and my father Abraham lived long lives as well. Though our family split apart, God was with us all!

# God Whispered in My Ear

*Written and Illustrated by Kathleen McKenzie*

## AUTHOR'S STATEMENT

GENESIS 22:1-19 *God Whispered in My Ear* is based on the Biblical story of the near-sacrifice of Isaac by his father, Abraham. I wrote it especially for children ages 7-12 who have experienced some form of trauma. By retelling this story from Isaac's perspective (that of a child caught up in a terrifying event beyond his ability to control or even understand), I hope to reassure children in similar circumstances that God will always be with them, no matter what happens. My prayer is that this story will also be used by caring adults to support children on their journey from trauma to healing.

KATHLEEN McKENZIE is a senior in the Master of Divinity program at McCormick Theological Seminary and is pursuing ordination as a Minister of the Word and Sacrament in the Presbyterian Church (U.S.A.). Prior to beginning seminary, Kathleen worked for many years as a master's-level social worker, serving children and families in and through their communities.

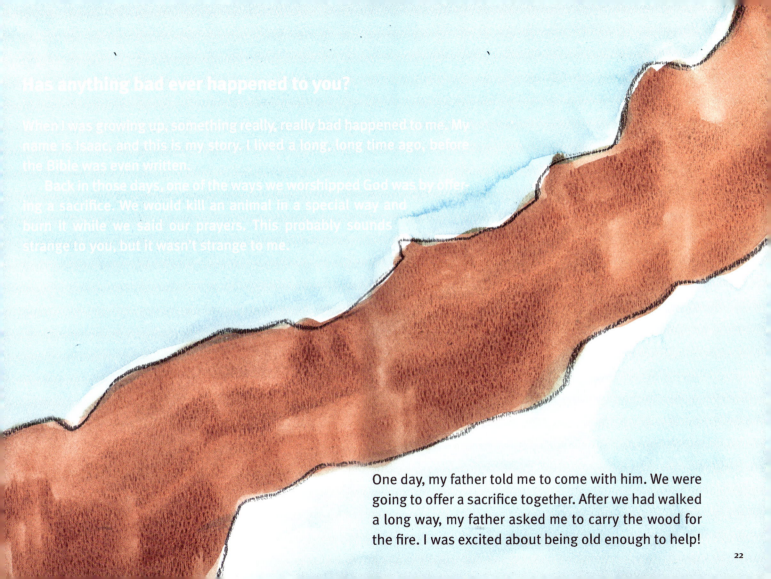

**Has anything bad ever happened to you?**

When I was growing up, something really, really bad happened to me. My name is Isaac, and this is my story. I lived a long, long time ago, before the Bible was even written.

Back in those days, one of the ways we worshipped God was by offering a sacrifice. We would kill an animal in a special way and burn it while we said our prayers. This probably sounds strange to you, but it wasn't strange to me.

One day, my father told me to come with him. We were going to offer a sacrifice together. After we had walked a long way, my father asked me to carry the wood for the fire. I was excited about being old enough to help!

22

When we were almost there, I realized that something was missing. Where was the animal for the sacrifice? My father told me not to worry; God would provide an animal. I didn't ask any more questions, but I had a strange feeling in my stomach.

I thought that something was wrong, and it was. When we arrived, my father tied me up and put me on the altar, the place where the animal for the sacrifice is killed. He took out his knife: Was he going to kill **ME** instead of an animal?

I was too scared to speak or even cry. I felt all alone. Just then, God whispered in my ear. God said: "Isaac, even though you cannot see me, I am right here with you. I will not leave you, no matter what happens."

Next, I heard the sound of an animal and saw a ram caught in a bush. My father untied me and took me off the altar. I stood and watched while he sacrificed the ram. Afterwards, he cried and said he was sorry. He didn't want to hurt me; he was just trying to obey God in the best way he knew how.

I believed him, but nothing was the same after that. I tried not to think about it, but I couldn't forget what had happened. At night, I sat up in my bed and wondered: "Why did this have to happen? What if it happens again?"

In the darkness, God whispered in my ear: "Sometimes things happen that are just too hard for kids or even grownups to understand. But, I understand. And I want to help you feel safe and strong again."

At first, I just listened. Then, I started to whisper back. I told God how confused and angry I was. I asked God questions, like: "Was it my fault?" (God said "No!") Eventually, I started to worry less and laugh more.

Months and years went by, and I kept talking. Not just to God, but to other people. I told them about what had happened to me and they told me about things that had happened to them. I learned that lots of bad things happen, but lots of good things happen too.

Now I am an adult, and my wife and I have two sons of our own. I still remember the really, really bad thing that happened to me when I was a child, but I don't think about it very much any more—except for when bad things happen to other kids.

Has anything bad ever happened to you?

God is right here with you, waiting to whisper in your ear.

What will you whisper back?

# One Sister's Choice

*by Erica Je' Taun McCullough*

## AUTHOR'S STATEMENT

GENESIS 37:12-36 My adaptation of the story of Joseph and his brothers is a real life experience for many young people today. Sibling rivalry is a common phenomenon that many children can relate to. This story was written for children ages 10-14 with no specific cultural or religious background in mind.

After reading and discussing *One Sister's Choice,* my desire is that children will understand that their emotions are normal, discover positive ways to cope and learn how to reconcile with individuals they are in conflict with. As a contemporary story, I retell it from the voice of the older sibling and allow her to wrestle deeply with her feelings. Additionally, I've added reflection questions in the beginning and end of the story for further processing.

ERICA JE'TAUN MCCULLOUGH is a resident of the South Side of Chicago and a senior at McCormick Theological Seminary. She serves in ministry at Prayer and Faith Outreach Ministries, a Non-Denominational congregation. After graduation, Erica will continue to serve in leadership at her home church and later pursue a Doctorate degree in hopes of teaching at a seminary.

*Artwork for* One Sister's Choice *was illustrated by Rodney Thomas.*

**Have you ever had a fight** with a sister, brother, or a friend? How did you respond? What did you do? How would you handle the situation differently next time? Think about this as I tell you a story about my brother and me.

This is how it all began...

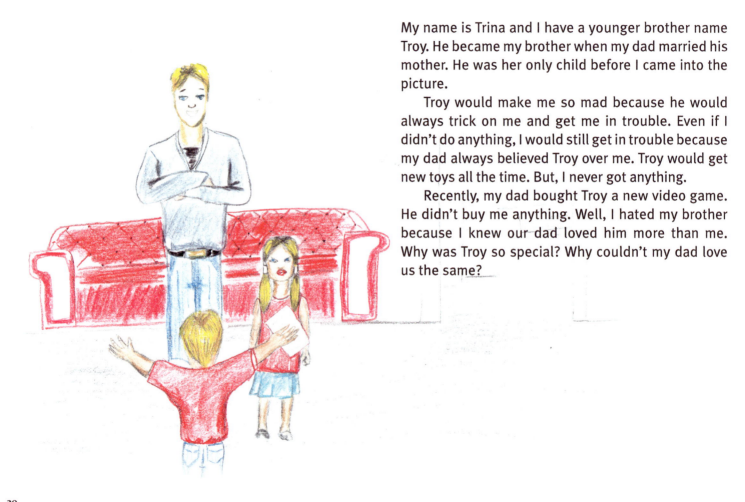

My name is Trina and I have a younger brother name Troy. He became my brother when my dad married his mother. He was her only child before I came into the picture.

Troy would make me so mad because he would always trick on me and get me in trouble. Even if I didn't do anything, I would still get in trouble because my dad always believed Troy over me. Troy would get new toys all the time. But, I never got anything.

Recently, my dad bought Troy a new video game. He didn't buy me anything. Well, I hated my brother because I knew our dad loved him more than me. Why was Troy so special? Why couldn't my dad love us the same?

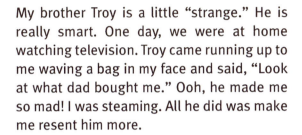

My brother Troy is a little "strange." He is really smart. One day, we were at home watching television. Troy came running up to me waving a bag in my face and said, "Look at what dad bought me." Ooh, he made me so mad! I was steaming. All he did was make me resent him more.

Another time, Troy came home from football practice jumping and screaming. Dad and I were talking in the kitchen. Troy got his grades and was all worked up because he got straight A's. He was bragging and making me feel like he was better than me.

He told me, "You're dumb, you didn't get all A's like me." I couldn't believe he said that to me.

I actually got a little jealous and envied him. My heart was so full of anger and resentment. "It's okay to feel this way," I said to myself.

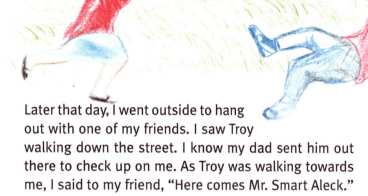

to hurt him! I thought about throwing him in front of a car. How smart will he be then? I could tell my dad that he ran across the street and got hit by a car.

I quickly thought about it. I hated my brother, but did I really want him to get hurt? Besides, I couldn't let my dad down anymore like I had done in the past. I'm Troy's big sister and I'm supposed to protect him, I thought. Anyway, I kept thinking about all the stuff he did to me... how angry I was...how much I despised him...I knew that it was ok for me to feel this way. But, what was I going to do?

Later that day, I went outside to hang out with one of my friends. I saw Troy walking down the street. I know my dad sent him out there to check up on me. As Troy was walking towards me, I said to my friend, "Here comes Mr. Smart Aleck." At that point, I wanted to do something to him! I wanted

With all those negative feelings that I had, I had to stop and think. I had a choice to make. I couldn't make a quick decision based on how I was feeling though. I couldn't hurt my brother so I thought, "Maybe I'll just rough him up a little."

By the time Troy got to me, I grabbed him and he fell on the ground. Troy started crying. I started to feel really bad. I shouldn't have grabbed him or even touched him. What I did was wrong.

Now, I had to tell my dad what happened. I knew he would be mad at me for what I did. So, I took my brother home and explained what happened. I went in my room and began to think about it. I knew what I did was wrong and I thought about how I should've handled the whole situation differently. I know there is a better way to handle the situation with my brother.

This is the story about Troy and me. Later, I learned that it's a lot like the story of Joseph and his older brothers. **What do you think about what I did? How would you have handled this situation? What would you have done differently?**

# When Jacob Held God

by Lindsey Anderson

"God will stay in relationship, held to us, by a love that will not let God go."*

## AUTHOR'S STATEMENT

GENESIS 32:22-32 Much of my relationship with God, especially as a young person, felt like (and still feels like) a wrestling match. As young people discover new things about the world, complexities of our faith, questions about God that they can't answer and answers about God that they don't like, it can feel as though their grip on God suddenly slips, or God suddenly does a 'double leg takedown.' For many years I saw this story of Jacob as a metaphor for my own wrestling with God over realities of violence and injustice in our world. But, as I was in the beginning stages of this project, I heard about a speech that Walter Brueggemann gave and it sparked my imagination. Could it be that this face to face, tightly held, struggling wrestle with God breeds a depth of intimacy that we rarely recognize and even more rarely credit to our young people?

LINDSEY ANDERSON grew up and has lived all her life in metro Detroit until three years ago, when she moved to Chicago. She misses the trees and wide open spaces but, loving the hustle and bustle of people, she decided to stay a bit longer. Since graduating from McCormick Theological Seminary, Lindsey has begun a pastoral residency at Fair Oaks Presbyterian Church in Oak Park, IL. She spends her time hanging out with teenagers, working on very amateur found-art creations and perfecting her bread-baking skills. Most of the time, she is busy having her own wrestling match with vocational discernment.

* Paraphrased from Walter Brueggemann's address at the PC(USA) Covenant Network conference in 2008.

I waited alone for the terrible morning.     I could see he was afraid, as the light scattered across the plain. Darkness came but not sleep. I waited with him.

I imagined my brother's face twisted with rage and bitterness, swearing revenge; I remembered the tears in my father-in-law's eyes as I rode away from his house with all that was most important to him. Would death be waiting for us in the morning? Maybe I deserved it after all my deception, but not my family. What would happen to them? It felt like something was on top of me, pressing me into the earth. I pushed and turned but I could not move the weight, and I kept seeing the faces.

When his fears had reached a fever-pitch, when a world's worth of worry had gathered on his chest, I stepped in. I appeared, arms grabbing on to him, legs bearing up against his force, waist twisting in his hold. He grabbed back. We were locked, both struggling.

Suddenly, it was some**one** that I was writhing under. My fate had not waited for me to come to it; it was here, tonight. I jerked and pushed and struggled against the stranger.

But wait, there was something familiar here. I recognized some feeling, the strange memory of another night many years ago came to me. Was this the same night visitor from before? Now the fear moving my limbs was joined by confusion and strange desire. Even when it hurt, I could not let go. I didn't want to let go.

I could not let go. He was holding on with all his might, but there was something else holding me there. I could not break from the hold of love; I loved Jacob so much that it would not let me separate my self from him, even in this struggle.

He was burning with emotion, fear, shame, anger, need. There was a lot to be answered for, but instead we remained, struggling in a violent embrace, beyond words.

We wrestled that way all night until I finally said, "Haven't you had enough? It's almost morning."

"No." He replied and held on tighter. "I want to be blessed."

"From now on," I said, "you will be called Israel because we struggled together through this difficult night."

And he was blessed.

The stranger broke the silence of the struggle, I hadn't noticed the sun rising.

"Bless me" I told him and would not let go. Then he asked my name and I asked for his, "Do you have to ask?" the stranger replied, and that was it, in that second it all locked into place, I could see, it was God.

"Now your name will be 'Israel,'" he said. And I was blessed.

I released him then, and I could no longer see him, but I could still feel his hold on me, lighter now but there. A lingering pain, reassuring in a way, pulling down on my hip.

Tired from struggling we walked out into    leaning on one
the morning,    another.

# Mysteries on a Mountain

*by Aimee Melgar*

## AUTHOR'S STATEMENT

**MATTHEW 17:1-8** Sometimes we lose sight of God's ability to act in ways we will never be able to fully explain. The story of the transfiguration is a reminder that God does not have limits on what he is capable of doing. *Mysteries on a Mountain* is intended for children 9-11 from any faith background, though there is clear teaching about Jesus in the passage. My hope is that this story will help children begin to explore God's mysteries with a sense of excitement and imagination. Using Peter as the main character, the readers are able to journey with him and hear his feelings, emotions and questions as he witnesses all of the incredible, unexplainable mysteries on the mountain.

**AIMEE MELGAR** attends a non-denominational church. She is an M.Div student at McCormick wih plans to graduate in the spring of 2010. Upon graduation she would like to work in a non-profit or governmental institution advocating on behalf of just social laws and policies.

Mysteries on a Mountain *was illustrated by Dámaris Mendoza.*

How thunder makes a loud **BOOM** sound during storms?
Why cats are so soft to touch or why hugs can make you feel so happy?

## Do you ever think about...

How roses have such a beautiful smell?
Why eating watermelon on a hot, sunny day tastes so good?

## Do you ever imagine...

How God can answer the prayers of so many people?
Why God created little bugs?

Throughout history people have tried to answer some of these questions. Some of the answers remain mysteries. A long time ago, Peter, James, John and Jesus went on an adventure up a mountain. Peter wants to share with you the mysteries he encountered with his friends...

I felt myself wanting to run **really fast** up the mountain with my good friends Jesus, James and his brother John. I was so excited that Jesus invited US to go up the mountain with HIM, all by ourselves.

## What would we do?

Maybe we would play some fun games, eat together, pray or tell jokes!

## What would we see?

Maybe some of our other friends would meet us at the top!

While I was still dreaming about all the activities we might do with Jesus, something happened that is hard to explain in words:

## The face of Jesus changed right in front of us!

Have you ever tried looking into the sun but then have to look away because it is too bright? Jesus' face was actually glowing just like the sun!

Then, Jesus' clothes became so white that it was almost hard for us to see him! My clothes change color when I get them dirty after playing outside, but they have never turned white. This was even better than playing games!

41

You will never believe what happened next. Moses and Elijah appeared and were talking to Jesus! James, John and I have all heard about Moses and Elijah, but we had never seen them because they died a long time ago. I wish I could have asked them some questions.

I wanted to ask Moses how it felt to hear God's voice from a burning bush.

I was curious what it was like for Elijah to be taken up to heaven by the wind.

It would also have been nice to hear where they came from, but it did not feel like the moment to ask.

Instead, I asked Jesus if he wanted me to make three places for Moses, Elijah and Jesus to stay. After all, everyone needs a place to sleep.

All of a sudden, a bright cloud covered us. It wasn't the cloud that was so surprising, but a voice from the cloud actually started to speak! The voice said:

This is my son, whom I love. I am very happy with him. Listen to him!

What would you have done if you heard a voice from a cloud? What were we supposed to listen to?

James, John and I were really scared and we fell to the ground right after hearing the voice. Somehow we knew God was telling us something very important.

Jesus must have noticed that we were scared because he came over and touched us and told us not to be afraid. We felt a lot better and when I looked up it was only James, John, Jesus and I. Jesus was all alone with us.

How come birds and airplanes can fly... ...but I can't?

How do colors paint the sky when the sun goes down?

How can Jesus be God's son??

Walking down the mountain felt a little different from our walk up. I had a lot of questions about all the mysteries I saw. I wondered how Jesus' clothes could look so white. Could my clothes change to blue, my favorite color?

I thought about how Moses and Elijah appeared. If I wanted to talk to John one night, could he appear in my room? I imagined other places voices could come from. Could God talk through the food that I eat?

As one foot followed the other I realized that all these questions might not be answered because they are myster-ies. I realized that I was just part of something bigger than me, part of something amazing. I knew I would keep wondering...

...wondering how colors paint the sky when the sun goes down... Thinking about how airplanes and birds stay in the air when I can not... Imagining how Jesus is God's son.

Will you wonder, think and imagine God's mysteries with me?

44

# The Day Zugritzam was Worried

*by Brenton Earl Thompson*

## AUTHOR'S STATEMENT

**MATTHEW 6:25-33** A reality of the world today is that children have to deal with more issues that affect their own security and stability than in earlier years. These are scary things to children and they can be overwhelming. The message of *The Day Zugritzam was Worried* seeks to engage children about the anxiety and stress upon their lives and offer them support emotionally. This story is intended for all children ages 8-10 and also gives extra attention to children with blindness or visual impairments.

**BRENTON EARL THOMPSON** was born and raised in Texas where he is a member in the Presbyterian Church (U.S.A.). In 2009 he graduated with a Master of Divinity from McCormick Theological Seminary. He looks forward to parish ministry while focusing on building and supporting healthy worshiping communities.

**Who is Zugritzam?** Zugritzam looks just like you, except for one special thing: Zugritzam can talk to animals and plants just like we talk to each other.

One day in the park, Zugritzam asked Squirrel, "Can you tell me about the future?"

Squirrel asked, "What would you like to know about the future?"

Zugritzam replied, "Well, since I can't see the future how do I know I'll have food to eat or if I grow even more and I can't get any more clothes?"

Squirrel sat on Zugritzam's shoulder and said, "Let me tell you about my two friends Ms. Bird and Mr. Flower.

"Ms. Bird is the one who sings in the park. She makes you smile when you hear her. Ms. Bird does not worry about what she will eat. She is not able to grow food for herself but she eats berries and seeds. When she can't find these things, people give her food because they care about her.

"Mr. Flower is the one who you smell every time you come to the park. His clothes are as thin as paper and when he is in bloom his delicate petals flutter just like your clothes do in the wind. Mr. Flower cannot make his own clothes. The rain from the clouds and the light from the sun help take care of Mr. Flower so that he can be clothed in beauty.

"Zugritzam, you are important to the people who know you. Things happen sometimes and your neighbors, friends and even people you don't know can help you when you need it. You won't be forgotten. We are here to help when we can."

After Squirrel had finished talking, Zugritzam asked him, "So you don't think I need to worry about the future?"

"Not today! If you need anything, someone should help you."

"Thank you for your help Squirrel, you were there when I needed help," Zugritzam said as the frown began to turn into a smile.

# The Crumbs of the Feast

*by Cathy C. Hoop*

## AUTHOR'S STATEMENT

**MATTHEW 15:21-28** Does the author choose the story or does the story choose the author? The story of the Canaanite woman chose me. As a mother of teenage sons, I could feel the woman's longing. I am blessed with healthy children, but healthy children still have demons...and we all long for health and wholeness for our children.

Beyond that, the conflict in the story invites readers to explore Jesus' humanity and boundless compassion. It is a story of exclusion and inclusion, a theme that is with us always. While primarily relying on Matthew's version, I have borrowed from Mark as well. I have given the daughter a face and a name, and I thought she should use a furry companion.

**CATHY C. HOOP** has had the privilege of serving as Director of Children's Ministries for Second Presbyterian Church of Nashville, Tennessee. She is also an occassional preacher and curriculum writer. She is hoping to complete a Masters of Christian Education from the Presbyterian School of Christian Education in Richmond, Virginia in 2009.

**When Asherah found him,** crouched under an old ox cart, he was scrawny and ugly. Just skin and bones.

Asherah coaxed him out with her gentle voice and a bone her mother had been saving for the soup pot. He flopped down in the grass and began blissfully gnawing away. Before long, Asherah was sitting beside him, stroking his fur while he slept.

When her mother discovered what Asherah had done, she was not pleased. "We needed that bone, Asherah. Your dinner will not be very tasty without it. Keep him if you must, but do not give him the food from our table! Our crumbs will be a feast for him."

So the pup stayed.

"I think you should call him 'Og'" her mother suggested. "'Og' means 'gigantic!' It will give him some hope, poor little runt of a dog." It wasn't long before they discovered that this dog had the heart of a giant.

He slept at Asherah's feet each night and stayed close by her side each day. And whenever Asherah was sure her mother couldn't see, Og feasted on small scraps from Asherah's bowl.

Asherah had not had many happy moments before Og appeared. She had a sickness for which there was no cure. Sometimes she would fall down on the ground and her body would shake and shake and shake. Her mother would sit beside her, place her on her side, and patiently wait for the seizure to end. She knew Asherah would wake up and be okay. But their neighbors and friends were frightened. They thought Asherah had an evil spirit inside her. They told their children to stay away from Asherah.

But Og didn't care about evil spirits. Og only cared about Asherah. She taught him to roll over, to sit up, to speak. His tricks made her laugh. Sometimes she thought that Og laughed, too.

One evening, there was a tap at the door. It was a neighbor.

"I thought you might want to know. I've heard that a Jewish prophet has come to our village. They call him Jesus. They say he makes the blind to see and the lame to walk. Maybe he could help Asherah," she said as she quickly turned to go.

Could it be possible? Asherah's mother was afraid to hope. And why would a Jewish prophet want to help her? Why would his Jewish God care for her? If they didn't know this God, did this God know them?

The next thing Asherah knew she was rushing along behind her mother, down the dark streets of the village. Og stayed right at her heels, taking pleasure in this unexpected adventure. Her mother seemed frantic, as if she was searching for someone, or something. Suddenly her mother stopped, raised her head and began shouting, "Have mercy on me, Lord, Son of David. Have mercy on my daughter! Have mercy on me, Lord!"

A door opened and light poured onto the mother and child. Several men tumbled into the street. "What do you want?" "Why are you here?" they asked.

"I am looking for the prophet who can make the lame to walk and the blind to see. I need him to heal my Asherah."

"Go away, woman." one of the men said. "Go away. The rabbi is resting." And the men closed the door, taking the light with them.

Asherah's mother pounded on the door. "Son of David, have mercy on me!"

Once again the door opened. "Send her away," someone said. Another turned to her and said, "Look." He opened the door wider.

Asherah's mother saw a man sitting at a low table. He looked weary. She saw bread crumbs, fish bones, a half-eaten cluster of grapes. The man looked at her, then looked up at his friends and spoke, "I was sent only to the lost sheep of Israel. I was sent to save my people." Did she hear hesitation in his voice? Did she hear confusion? Why wouldn't he look at her??

Asherah's mother wiped the desperate tears from her eyes and grabbed Asherah in her arms. She rushed into the room and placed Asherah at the man's feet. "Lord, help me," she begged. Og ran in and stood protectively beside Asherah.

"I cannot take the children's food and throw it to the dogs," he answered.

At that moment, Asherah began to shake. The room was still except for Asherah. Og whimpered and licked Asherah's trembling hand.

"Is it a dog you see before you?" Asherah's mother asked, her voice trembling. "Even the dogs get the crumbs that fall from the master's table. The crumbs of the feast."

Immediately Jesus knelt down beside the now still girl. He placed a hand on Asherah's head. He stroked her hair. He looked into her mother's face. "Your faith amazes me," he said to her. "Your daughter is well."

Asherah's eyes fluttered open. "Never again, Asherah," said her mother, scooping her up into her arms. "Never again."

Asherah sat up. She began to laugh as she spied Og, standing in the middle of the table, noisily enjoying the crumbs of the master's feast.

**THE END.**

# Can I Make Peace?

*by Mark Schimmelpfennig*

### AUTHOR'S STATEMENT

**MATTHEW 17:1-8** Children today perhaps face the realities of war and conflict more acutely than in previous generations, given the real-time environments that television and the internet bring to their lives. Like any event that directly affects them, children need to be able to make sense of those events and know that God is with them through it all. This story is written from the perspective of a young boy whose father has been deployed to Iraq. He is simply trying to make sense of the realities that face him, and how he can cope with them with God's help. This story was written for 5-7 year olds.

**MARK SCHIMMELPFENNIG** is a member of the Presbyterian Church (U.S.A.), and graduated with an M.Div. degree from McCormick Theological Seminary in 2009. While Mark has lived all over the world, he calls Chicago, Illinois home. Mark is looking forward to a call in Parish Ministry, specializing in Mission and Outreach.

**I miss my dad a lot.** Lots of people are fighting and hurting each other in Iraq.

My dad has been over there for a long time now. He is there to help. My mom and my little brother miss him a lot too. It makes me sad sometimes.

My Sunday school teacher told us that Jesus said that peacemakers are blessed. God loves them very much. Our blessings come when we make peace. I know that blessings are really good things. They are special gifts from God. **If God blesses people who make peace, then why are so many people fighting all the time?**

I told my teacher that if I could, I would make peace right now. Then maybe my dad could come home. Maybe even in time for Christmas.

**But how can I make peace?** I am only six. Almost seven.

She said that there are still lots of ways I can be a peacemaker. That made me feel better.

She asked me to think of ways that I could make peace with my family and friends and at church. She said that peacemaking is more than stopping fights.

It sounded like a good idea. I thought REALLY, REALLY hard...

I promised not to hit my little brother anymore when he plays with my toys and steals my Matchbox cars. I would not argue with my mom to stay up past my bedtime. I promised not to make icky faces when I have to eat my green beans. **At first, peacemaking seemed like a lot of work. But I kept at it...**

I made friends with the new kids at school that no one wanted to talk to...I helped to stop two fights at recess. Those kids did not have to get grounded. I still DON'T like GREEN beans. That is going to take a while longer!

At church we do lots of things to help people who are poor. Who are hungry, or have nowhere to live. I think I would like to help. Helping all those people would be peacemaking wouldn't it? I think so.

**I wonder: If I am a peacemaker, will others try too?** I hope so. Then pretty soon, maybe the whole world will start making peace. Stop fighting and hurting each other. **God could bless the whole world for being peacemakers.** That would be cool.

Then maybe my dad could come home. That would make me glad.

# Betrayals

*Written and Illustrated by Anna Kendig*

## AUTHOR'S STATEMENT

**MATTHEW 26:17-27:10, SELECTED VERSES** When presented for children and youth, the story of the trial and death of Jesus is often simplified in a manner that polarizes the actions of flawed characters and the calm actions of Jesus. Yet issues of betrayal, loyalty, despair, and even suicide described in Matthew's gospel can speak to the experiences of teens. Retold from the perspective of the conflicted, confused disciples – namely the problematic and disgraced characters of Peter and Judas – this retelling seeks compassion and grace even in the midst of human sinfulness. To engage youth with the text, a poetic voice and a driving tone parallel the events accelerating toward one of the most somber spaces in the gospel. Yet even in these shadowed places, God sees human despair and frailty, and responds.

**ANNA KENDIG** is a native of Minnesota and a recent graduate of McCormick Theological Seminary in Chicago. Inheriting her faith from her Mexican Presbyterian heritage, she has also been influenced by her father's love of philosophy. She loves the act of worshipping and storytelling in Christian community and hopes for a vital, welcoming parish ministry in the years to come.

# [The Table]

Room prepared, food ready, sun's last fire fading on the hills. Eating together, each one talking, Jesus laughing, listening, loving each one. Good times, good memories, warmth and trust together. Everything feels good and right. Without warning, a prediction:

Jesus says, "One of you will turn me in to those who hate me; you will betray me."

Everything stops. Everyone stunned, lost. What? It can't be true... but each has been afraid, each has had doubts.... Still, no one would go that far. Jesus must be wrong...

But each asks (just in case!): "It's not me, Lord?" and, "Will it be me?"

Judas keeps eating, quiet, thinking; dipping his bread into the bowl.

Jesus says, "The one who has just dipped his bread in this bowl with me is the one who will betray."

*Everyone looks at Judas.*

And Jesus says, "This is what the prophets predicted for me, but the choice is still his. To hand over the one who has come to save... it would have been better if he had never even been born."

Judas speaks then – softly, softly – "It's not me, Teacher?"

Jesus says, "That's what you say." Ugly silence. But then Jesus surprises again: a smile. Sadness still in his eyes, looking around the table, noting each and every one, and smiling, just smiling and full of love. Hearts ease.

Slowly, Jesus takes bread. Blesses, breaks, and gives it to pass around. He says, "Take this. Eat it. This bread is me. My body." Means what? No one knows, but the silence feels holy now. The bread tastes the same, but feels different to eat.

Jesus picks up a cup, blesses, and says, "Drink this. This is my life. My blood, which is the covenant promise. It's given now for forgiveness. I will drink again with you on the New Day coming, when God's love will cover all things."

Each drinks. From the one cup. Strange, strange peace fills their bodies. And they break into song together, right there, in praise to the God of love.

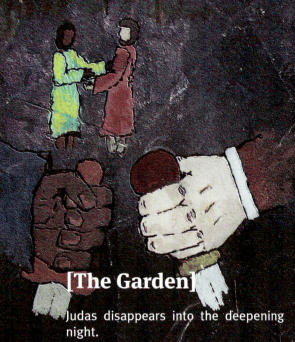

## [The Garden]

Judas disappears into the deepening night.

Everyone walking toward the Mount of Olives. Jesus getting quieter and quieter. He stops. Says suddenly: "All of you will desert me tonight, because of what's about to happen. You will scatter. You will fall away.'"

"What?!" everyone's asking. More surprises. Peter blurts, loud, "I swear I never will."

Jesus looks at Peter, eyes mysterious, "Tonight, exactly tonight, before the rooster crows, you will betray me three times."

Insistent Peter: "Not me, Lord! Even if I have to die with you, I will never disown you." Everyone agrees with him, meaning every word. All are ready to die standing with their great friend.

Jesus gets sadder, quieter. Turning to them all: "I must pray alone. But stay. Be awake with me; pray for me." He goes off. Soon, their tired eyes find sleep. Time and again, Jesus comes back and asks for prayer, but they can't keep sleep-weighted eyes open.

Jesus returns again, saying urgently, "Wake up! The time is now. I am about to be handed over to those who will act in ugliness and fear. Get up and let's go: my betrayer is here."

Crashing through the trees, then, the footsteps of a crowd. Judas in their midst, avoiding the eyes of his friends. Disciples confused, groggy, ready for a fight. Judas approaches Jesus, lays his hand on his shoulders, and kisses his cheek. "Greetings, Teacher." he says, quietly, looking Jesus in the eyes.

Jesus asks him, gently, "Why do you do this, my friend?" But no time to respond. Hands appear, guards grabbing, grasping, tying Jesus with rope. The disciples' swords appear, wielded in anger and defense.

"NO!" comes the shout. Jesus' yell halts everyone. "Put away violence. Put away fear and anger. They will only destroy you. I will go in peace, because I know the power of my Father, and the power of the truth that is going to be revealed. Let the prophecies come true."

Too much confusion for the disciples. Too many prophecies, too much danger. Too many hopes suddenly lost. Confused and afraid, all the friends flee into the night, leaving Jesus alone.

# [The Temple]

Peter, running away madly through the trees. Gasping for breath, grasping at hope. Maybe, maybe Jesus will defend himself. Maybe he will escape. Maybe. Then a thought: Jesus would never run.

So Peter stops. And turns. Follows softly behind the crowd. Watches as Jesus is shoved into the courtyard, where only angry voices and Jesus' calm tone can be heard. Peter, straining to hear, warms his fright-cold hands at the communal fire. He suddenly feels old and haggard. Empty and terrified. This must be a nightmare.

Curious faces look at him. He ignores. What do they matter, now? But a young girl speaks up, calmly. "I know you. You're one of the friends of Jesus of Galilee."

"You make no sense." says Peter, quickly, retreating further behind the hood of his cloak. He moves away from the fire to the colder gateway.

Another pesky servant-girl. This one brazen, accusing: "This man is friends with Jesus of Nazareth."

"No! I don't even know him!" Peter backing away from the gathered crowd, footsteps stumbling, unsure. He finds a corner where he can be alone. Cloaked in shadows, brooding, eyes darting. Who will accuse him next? How can he stay in such danger... but how can he desert Jesus? Jesus had called him a friend, the "steady rock," and promised so many great things for his future... But all that seems lost now.

Another one approaches, teasing, nasty, "I know you're one of those friends of his. You come from his country and talk the same way."

Words pour out before thought can stop them: "No, no, NO! I swear to you all: may I be cursed if I even knew him at all. I don't know that man." Yelling, yelling, making a scene – it's not safe. Now all the guards are looking. If they find out, they'll arrest him, too...

The crowd closes tighter around him, but all are distracted by a loud sound: a rooster crowing. Just outside the gate. And Jesus' words flood back: Peter's vow, the denials, the rooster's crow. It came true, it all came true. No time to think now, the guards might come over to ask questions. Peter turns. And runs.

Jesus captured. Friends gone. Vow broken. How did it come to this? Collapsed outside, safe in an alley with the smell of trash and the sounds of rats digging around, Peter weeps. Face mashed, eyes shut, can't stop crying. Picks up a stone, throws it away bitterly. Thinks: how could a shattered, misshapen stone be the foundation of anything?

Near the rooftop, a bird begins to sing.

# [The Field]

Morning just beginning to dust brightness on the dark eastern sky. City still sleeping, except for the priests and elders, up all night putting Jesus to trial. Final verdict: death.

Judas hears the word, passed through whispers and shouts. The money bag still hidden in his cloak heavy, heavy like it's dragging him under the earth. Burning his skin where it touches, a sign of death. How has it come to this?

He drags himself inside the temple, confronts the chief priests and elders. They look, but do they even recognize him? The man who helped their plan?

"Take it back, take it back, take it back," he cries. "Such a terrible thing, and I did it. I turned him in. But I know that man, and he is innocent."

"No matter, doesn't matter," say the chief priests, ignoring his words. "The decision is made: he will die. And you will be rich." Sneers all around. They walk away.

Judas yelling at their retreating backs, "No, no, NO! I take it back. I refuse the money! I take it back. Take your money." Alone in the echoing room, Judas throws the coins to the temple floor. They roll out of the bag, winking silver in the lantern light, scattering on the stones.

Judas running, running. To nowhere. Anywhere. Away, away. Thinking: What have I done? How did it come to this? Murderer, betrayer, thief, traitor, evil monster... the words revolve in his head – ugly song with no start and no end. No space for anything else.

Finds himself, suddenly, on the edge of the city, in a field. Open expanses, air. Birds call to one another, wind moves the grain in the field.

He falls kneeling at the base of a tree, alone, so alone. O God, O God, where are you now? I am lost.

Hours later, Judas is found. Hanged from a tree, despairing of grace. The priests gather the coins from the temple floor and buy the field where he was found, calling it the Field of Blood. They think the story is over.

But no one saw the single budded leaf on that last tree, no one heard the bird in the air, calling "here, here..."

No one remembered the gentle hands that lifted Judas and let him rest from agony at last.

# whisper, shout

*by Kristin Hollenbach*

### AUTHOR'S STATEMENT

MATTHEW 28:1-10 this story is unabashedly and unapologetically written to lift up the witness of women who carry a message of hope and justice through time and space.

KRISTIN HOLLENBACH asks a lot of questions. she is not content settling for the same old story. she dances. bakes bread. and can spend hours at the farmer's market or thrift store. kristin lives in chicago with her partner, seven housemates, four cats, two dogs and a wild garden.

Morning just beginning to dust brightness on the dark horizon. City still sleeping, except for Mary and Mary, up so early coming to see the tomb. Silence, except for the hushed whisper of a bird's feather. Stillness, except for a leaf's timid dance.

They watched him. Being buried here. Cannot stop remembering the nightmare—the nails, his cries, his final breath. Nothing they could have done. Powerless. Even now. Here. At the tomb. Where they are supposed to be. But it doesn't matter. They don't matter. They are women. Voiceless. Excluded.

Jesus. Gone. Lost.

O God, O God where are you now?

Sudden earth rumbling.

Earth groaning, now quaking! Terrified guards tremble, crumbling to the ground. Thundering. Stone rolling, angel descending, Mary and Mary squinting in white lightning gleam of snow-white clothing. Blindly clutching each other, cowering, desperate.

*Don't be afraid.*

*I know you are looking for Jesus. He is
not here; he has been raised.*

Raised?

*Come, see the place where he was.*

They watched him being buried here, they saw!  But he is gone.

*Go and tell his disciples, "He has been
raised from the dead."*

Raised!

*He's going to Galilee; you will see him
there.*

Jesus had said this to all of them, at their last supper together, when they had
broken bread and laughed and listened and loved together, when they had
known warmth and trust. When he had known he would be betrayed. When he
said they would all scatter and fall away. When he said they would see him again
in Galilee. Everything had happened as he said.

Only Mary and Mary remained. Just two women. Alone.
*No one else.*

Grabbing Mary's trembling hand, they run into the mourning sun, wiping tears from their smiling, confused faces. They cannot believe what they have heard, cannot imagine all they have seen, but, quickly, they must tell everyone!

*Sisters!*

They hear the voice before they see him, they hear that voice above the pounding of their sandals on the pathway and the fullness of nothing in their heads.

Jesus! It is he!

It is you! They run to him, throwing their arms around him. They weep, as if tears had power enough to heal.

*Don't be afraid.*

How could they be afraid? Jesus is here, looking in their eyes, wrapped in their embrace. The same Jesus who shared so many meals of bread, fish, and wine. The same Jesus who touched sick people when everyone else ignored them. The same Jesus who had helped blind people see the beauty of the world again. The same Jesus who loved the poor, the stranger, the rejected when no one else would. How could they be afraid?

*Go tell my brothers to go to Galilee;*
*they will see me there.*

Mary and Mary ran.

They ran telling everyone that Jesus was alive again.

**Sometimes they shouted,** sometimes they had to whisper.

They whispered in the villages on the way;
they shouted when they reached the disciples in Galilee.

And then they kept running, shouting and whispering...

| | |
|---|---|
| They shouted to Priscilla, | whispered to Lydia. |
| They shouted to Sojourner Truth, | whispered to Harriet Tubman. |
| Shouted to Jane Addams | whispered to Mother Teresa. |
| Shouted to Rosa Parks, | whispered to Dolores Huerta. |
| Shouted to Joan Baez, | whispered to Gloria Anzaldua. |
| Shouted to Audre Lorde, | whispered to Maxine Hong-Kingston. |
| Shouted to Irene Adelaide Greenwood, | whispered to Rigoberta Menchu Tum. |
| Shouted to Hina Jilan, | whispered to Mahar Nassa. |
| Shouted to Liza Maza, | whispered to Tikva Honig-Parnass. |
| Shouted to Ela Gandhi, | whispered to Vandana Shiva. |
| They are shouting even today | to women and men all over the world. |

**They are whispering to you.**